SEX PLAY

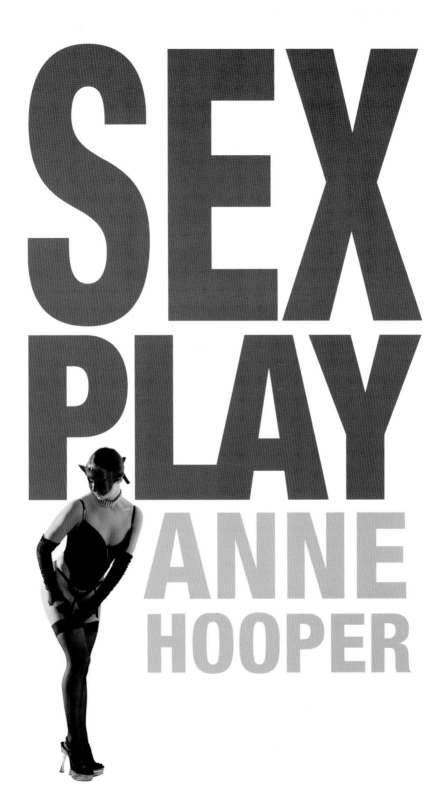

ANNE HOOPER

SEX PLAY

ANNE HOOPER

DK

London, New York, Munich, Melbourne, Delhi

Editor Kesta Desmond
Designer Phil Gamble
Photography Direction Lynne Brown
Senior Editor Simon Tuite
Senior Art Editor Helen Spencer
DTP Designer Traci Salter
Production Controller Clare McLean
Executive Managing Editor Adèle Hayward
Managing Art Editor Nick Harris
Art Director Peter Luff
Publisher Corinne Roberts

This edition first published in the United Kingdom
in 2006 by Dorling Kindersley Limited,
80 Strand, London WC2R 0RL

THE PENGUIN GROUP

2 4 6 8 10 9 7 5 3 1

A CIP catalogue record for this book is available from
the British Library

ISBN-13: 978-1-4053-1748-1
ISBN-10: 1-4053-1748-5

SD234

Colour reproduction by Colourscan, Singapore
Printed and bound in Singapore by Star Standard

See our complete catalogue at
www.dk.com

Contents

Hot fashion 10

Games and fantasies 50

Erotic treats 76

 Pushing back the boundaries 120

 Sex and shopping 162

Introduction

Today sex is experienced not just as a private activity between two people, but also as a statement of lifestyle and fashion. It's younger lovers who are leading the way in this style revolution. Sex Play is intended to appeal to all loving couples who fancy moving onto the slightly more adventurous sides of love, but in a way that feels safe and unthreatening.

If you like the idea of dressing up for sex, you'll find plenty of inspiration in Chapter 1. Whether you see yourself as a vamp, a virgin, or a goth, there are plenty of style tips. You can even be fashionable when you're naked by styling your pubic hair or decorating your skin with a temporary tattoo

Chapter 2 is for game players. Sex games are a fantastic antidote to sexual boredom – they can turn ordinary lovemaking into something exciting and charged with sexual tension. Taking on different roles, acting out erotic fantasies and using sexy props can really turn up the heat in your sex life. I've suggested a range of games from fantasy roleplay to kinky rubber games.

In Chapter 3 I've explored the world of erotic treats – if you've ever wondered how to give a Tantric sex massage, give someone an orgasm on the phone, or stimulate your lover's body using just your teeth, this is the place to find out. And if you want to push your sexual boundaries further, turn to Chapter 4. Here you can discover how to strip like a professional, shoot your own porn, and throw the sex party that none of your guests will forget.

The final chapter will help you become an expert when it comes to choosing and using erotic toys. Today, people are more open to the idea of experimentation in bed and there is a corresponding growth in sex aids and novelties. More and more, sex toys and DVDs are being sold amidst ordinary items on sale all the time. The internet has made sex toys incredibly easy to access and buy. Although women are buying many erotic novelties, every sex item bought by a woman also gets scrutinized by the man in her life. So whether you are a man or a woman, it's useful to know your way around the world of pumps, straps, rings, beads, dildos, and vibrators.

Throughout Sex Play I have included erotic interviews and quizzes – these are intended as fun ways to help you find out about you and your lover's sexual tastes and aspirations. I've also included some candid first-

person accounts of how couples or individuals have tried
something new sexually and the impact it had on their
sex lives. I believe that sex is one area of life in which two
trusting adults can truly relax, let their guard down, and
throw themselves into the sensuality and eroticism of play.
If you've never tried something before, don't worry about
looking silly. Make a revolution with your lover, do throw
away your inhibitions. You only goal are to explore,
experiment, and – above all – to have fun.

Anne Hooper

Hot fashion

The way you dress is a kind of sexual semaphore. You can send out a different message (everything from virgin to vamp) with each different outfit you choose. Clothes don't just transform your physical appearance – they change your behaviour too. As soon as you put on a sexy costume, you may find yourself effortlessly acting the part of the siren or the seducer. Try it out and see what happens.

EROTIC INTERVIEW

Explore your lover's tastes in erotic fashion by asking them the following questions. There are no right or wrong answers. The questions are simply for fun – and to help you get a really good picture of what turns your lover on.

1 Which word best describes your taste in underwear: kinky, cute, glamorous, sluttish, or sporty?

2 Which do you prefer: to look at others or for others to look at you?

3 If I strip for you, what would you most like me to wear underneath my clothes?

4 What's better: stripping off for sex or dressing up for sex?

5 If we were dressing up to go to a fetish party, what kind of outfit would we wear?

6 Imagine I'm waiting in bed for you when you get home from work. You slowly pull back the sheet. What am I wearing?

7 Imagine we're going clothes shopping together. Would we go to a normal department store, an erotic lingerie shop, or a website that specializes in outrageously kinky fetish gear?

What did you discover about your lover? Are they a closet fetishist? Did you uncover a secret passion for leather or PVC underwear? Or is your lover as happy with simple nudity as a kinky costume? Now it's your turn to answer the same questions!

These are dramatic costumes for making dramatic statements – try one out next time you go to a party. The message is loud and clear: "Look at me! And keep looking!" Don't be scared of dressing up to the max. And, whatever you wear, wear it with brazen confidence.

Drama queens

Goth girl

Her skin is deathly white but her face is illuminated by her crimson lips. Her tight, black clothes reveal the outline of her body. Her hands are encased in dark, slinky gloves, and her nails, painted red or black, are designed for scratching. She's not afraid of the darker side of sex and seduction. You can tell by her unflinching gaze that she knows just what she wants and how she's going to get it.

Medieval maiden

With her long dress, flowing robes, and long, streaming hair she radiates virginal innocence. She looks as though she's just floated across the forest clearing. Her romantic costume brings to mind thoughts of knights, chivalry, war, and the ravishing of maidens – one maiden in particular. She may be wearing a chastity belt but

Sex kitten

There's something effortlessly sexy and school-girlish about her — perhaps she's even dressed in school uniform. Is it her short skirt, her glossy pink lips, her smooth skin, her long eyelashes, or the way the pretty top seems to just slide off her shoulder? Or is it her sexy body language? Everything she does seems loaded with an erotic charge, whether it's the way she crosses her legs and leans forward, the way she bends over, or the cute way she gazes at you, as though she thinks you're amazing? Unlike the goth girl, the sex kitten wears colours that are bright and bubbly. Choose pinks, reds, and yellows.

Is it her short skirt, her glossy pink lips, or the way the top slides off her shoulder?

Rockabilly queen

She might be wearing a figure-hugging halter-neck dress, a bikini top and skirt, or ultra-tight pedal pushers. Her hair may be dyed a flamboyant pink and swept back in a pony tail. She almost certainly has a cute fringe. There's a life and verve to a rockabilly queen that makes you just want to get out there and party. Of course dancing (really hard dancing) gets up a sweat, and when you get too hot you just have to take off some clothes.

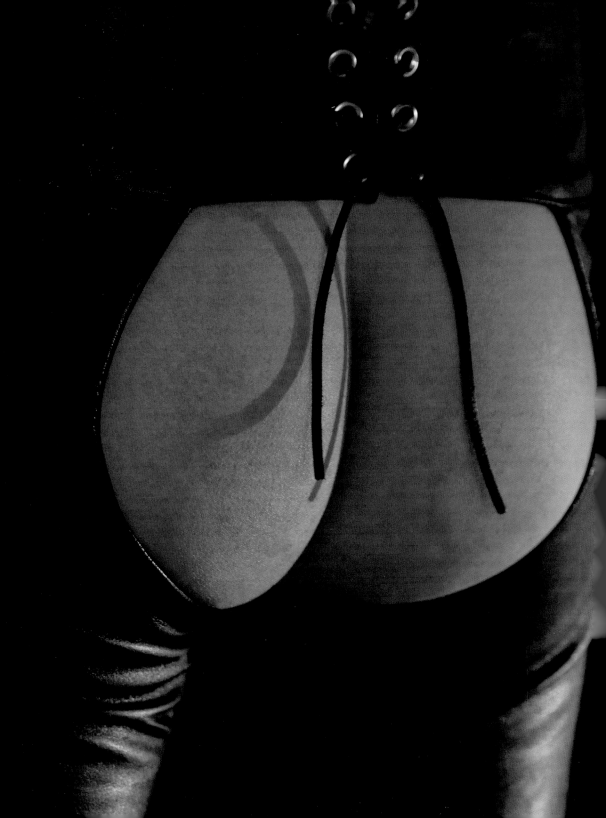

Rude costumes

Sometimes, dressing sexily involves out-and-out exhibitionism. The aim is to reveal and flaunt. Showing-it-all-off outfits are perfect for sexy parties, clubs, or for the delight of your lover in the privacy of your bedroom. Warning: rude costumes are not for the shy.

For the girls:

◆ A skimpy skirt or a pair of shorts, a black, red, or pink feather boa – and absolutely nothing else.

◆ Micro bikini bottoms and self-adhesive nipple covers.

◆ A front-zip catsuit with the zip undone to the navel.

◆ A corset that ends just beneath the breasts.

◆ A latex dress that laces up from behind – and strictly no underwear.

For the boys:

◆ Leather or PVC trousers with the behind cut out.

◆ A PVC apron with nothing on underneath.

◆ A leather jock strap and a collar.

◆ Jeans ripped around the crotch and a tight vest.

◆ A policeman's hat and some tight black shorts.

The art of rude dressing

Rude costumes are all about attracting attention to the sexiest parts of your body. Here's how to pull it off:

- Whether you're a man or a woman, the first thing is to decide upon your best physical asset. For example, is it your pert or voluptuous breasts, your smooth buttocks, your toned belly, your strong arms, or your long, slim legs? If you're not sure, ask a friend or lover. In fact, ask a friend or a lover anyway: a second opinion can help to bolster your confidence. Now choose a costume that best reveals this part of your body.

- Make sure the exposed bit of your body is in tip-top condition. The more kissable and strokeable it looks, the more admiring glances you're likely to receive. So cleanse, exfoliate, and wax if necessary. Skin with a healthy, brown glow looks good, so slap on some self-tanning lotion.

- Walk with confidence. A rude costume only needs to be worn with plenty of attitude. Hold your head up and keep your body language strong and open. If you feel nervous at first, and want some anonymity, wear a pair of shades.

- If you're going virtually nude, it's a good idea to leave at least one thing hidden so that people have something to guess about (and your lover has a part of your body to unwrap or uncover when you get into bed). If you're a woman, try covering your nipples. Use adhesive nipple covers. They come in a variety of shapes from the pretty, such as flowers and butterflies, to the saucy, such as lips, flames, and pairs of hands.

For men, dressing up as the opposite sex can help to liberate their softer side. Likewise, women can find that a traditionally male outfit brings out their tougher traits. Try swapping genders for a day and see what effect it has on what you say and do, and – most interesting of all – how it affects the way you have sex. You may find you end up swapping roles in bed too.

Change sex for a day

Drag king dress

Dress in your lover's shirts and trousers. If his trousers are too big,

Drag king attitude

Change your posture and body language. Sit with your legs wide apart rather than crossing them. Place your feet flat on the ground. When you stand up, take your time and lean forward before straightening up. When walking, let the action come from the top half of your body. Don't wiggle your hips or buttocks. Let your weight fall first to one side and then the other. Make your strides longer than usual and don't give an inch to anyone who comes into your personal space. Let your voice drop to its lowest natural pitch.

Drag queen dress

Dress in skirt, tights, and blouse (or a dress) – your lover's if you can get into them. Make sure you are clean-shaven and apply moisturizer and foundation to your skin. Follow this with mascara on your eyelashes and a coat of lipstick on your lips. Practise walking in high heels. Take much smaller steps than you would do normally.

Drag queen attitude

Speed up your body movements and be more expressive in your body language – in particular, use your hands to express your thoughts and feelings. Deliberately heighten your voice so that it hits an upper register. Generally be more playful. It's interesting to note that transsexual men become far more feminine and convincing women by adapting their body movements and tone of voice than by going for expensive cosmetic surgery.

Sex change for two

Who's in charge in your relationship? If he always plays the
sexual predator and she always plays passive, try swapping
roles for the night. Take on all the trappings of your lover's
gender, from dress to sexual behaviour. Here's how one

"Just wearing man's clothes made me feel strong and dominant."

"I suggested that we swap clothes and roles for the evening. The act
of putting make-up on my boyfriend and dressing him in my clothes
was funny at first, but it was also quite sexy and exciting. He seemed
to get really into it – he showed me how to put his tie on, and he got
out one of his smart suits. I wore the jacket and the trousers – and
nothing underneath. I liked the broad shoulders of the jacket and the
feeling of the silky lining against my nipples. I've got shoulder-length
hair that I always wear loose, but I tied it back. Just making these
changes made me feel strong and dominant. I even spoke differently –
I commanded my boyfriend to do things rather than asking him.

Then my boyfriend surprised me by telling me he'd bought me a present. He's bought me underwear and sex toys before, but nothing like this – it was a harness and a strap-on dildo. He pulled down my trousers and we fixed it in place together.

Then my boyfriend stepped back. It was clear from this point on that he was going to be passive and let me take control of what happened. I was really turned on. I licked, kissed, and bit him all over his body. He'd had an erection for quite a while by this stage but I decided to tease him by not going anywhere near his penis.

I've never worn a dildo before and it felt strange. It definitely gave me a feeling of being in charge. It also had an effect on the kinds of movements I made. I found my pelvis spontaneously thrusting against my boyfriend. I put some lube on the dildo and told my boyfriend to

"I found my pelvis spontaneously thrusting against him."

turn around so that he had his back to me. I couldn't quite bring myself to penetrate him (maybe I'll do that next time!) but I did lots of rubbing and thrusting which was fantastic for both of us.

The thing I enjoyed most was how turned on I got by the role reversal. I really loved the feeling of sexual power. I didn't feel self-conscious in the way that I thought I might. And my boyfriend was able to be receptive and vulnerable – two qualities that don't come very naturally to him. It was exciting to a see a different side of each other."

If you want to dress up as a couple, try the vamped-up gothic look. Goth lovers look slinky, seductive, and unapproachably sexy. This is a late-at-night look for dark rooms and dark nights. Even when everyone else is going home to bed, you just know that you and your lover will be up until dawn.

Graveyard shift

As a goth woman, you'll be wearing a long, tight, black dress with a neckline that plunges to reveal the dead white skin of your chest and breasts. Your neck will be decorated with a black choker or some ornate jewellery that leads the eye to your cleavage. Your legs will be encased in black spider-web tights. Your make-up is black. As a goth man, you'll be dressed in black with a splash of red. You'll be wearing black lipstick and eye makeup too. Essential goth accessories for both of you: white face powder, coloured contact lenses, fake blood, fangs, and – for when you get home – black condoms.

Your tight black dress plunges to reveal the dead white skin of your chest and breasts.

Heel power

Take a tip from the porn stars and beg, borrow, or steal a pair of hooker-style high heels. They will boost your confidence as well as your height. Lap and pole dancers wear them partly for their sexy, glamorous appearance, and partly because they give you a trademark hip-sway as you walk.

Take a tip from the porn stars and beg, borrow, or steal a pair of hooker-style high heels

Seduce your lover wearing nothing but your heels, fishnet tights or stockings, and a short skirt or a pair of shorts. Men—you can do this too! Play up your role to the max by standing with one foot on a chair, sexily unrolling your stockings, or playfully resting your heel on your lover's thigh, crotch, or chest. If roleplay turns you on, pretend you are a pole dancer auditioning for a job. Your lover is the demanding owner of an exotic dancing club. You're desperate for the job, so you're prepared to do almost anything but not without teasing them along the way. Keep your heels on during sex—even if everything else comes off.

body shape and definition. Shop around and see which garments maximize the bits you're proud of and minimize the bits you're not.

Body Sculpting

Leather, PVC, latex, and vinyl clothes are widely available from sex shops or websites. Search for "fetish wear" on the internet. Try

Roleplay for her

Imagine that you are a grand lady struggling into your underclothes. Enlist your lover's help to get dressed. His role is to be your faithful servant and his job is not only to hook, zip, lace, or strap you into your garments, but to stimulate your body as he goes. As he caresses your breasts and buttocks, you struggle to contain your pleasure. When he has finished dressing you, you make the decision as to whether you will reward his servile efforts.

His job is not only to hook, zip, lace, or strap you in, but to stimulate you as he goes.

Roleplay for him

Imagine that you are the leather-clad biker and you're rough and tough in your demands. Lay out your gear on the bed and ask her to dress you. After your lover has carefully zipped, buckled, and strapped you into your leather gear, you decide to seduce her.

Your role is to be dominant – pick her up, press her to the wall, and kiss her. When you're both at the peak of arousal, make love to her. Don't bother to get into bed. Have spontaneous sex in which she leans across the back of or over the arm of a chair.

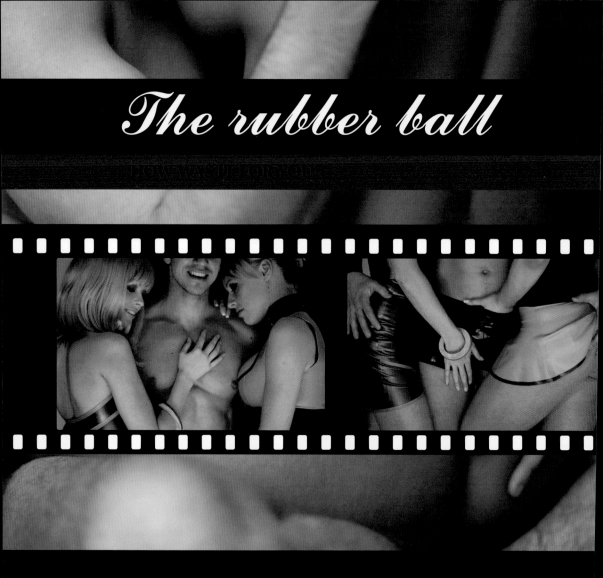

The rubber ball

If you love dressing up and you have an exhibitionist streak, you'll be in your element at a fetish club. Different club nights have different themes – everything from spanking to swinging – so check first that the theme is to your taste. Here's an account from a couple who went to a rubber ball.

"I thought my latex outfit was daring, but there were lots more outrageous costumes."

"We both went dressed in latex. We walked into a huge marquee. My first impression was how dark it was. But then we got used to the dim light and we started exploring. The marquee had lots of partitions and spooky little hidey-holes. There was a central dance floor full of people dressed in extraordinary costumes.

People seemed to be parading rather than actually dancing. I thought my latex outfit was daring, but there were lots more outrageous costumes. There were quite a few naked people as well. People came up to us quite freely to look, flirt, and touch.

their men on leads. Some people went around on all fours. Quite a few people had black rubber masks on their heads so that you couldn't see their faces.

We went into one room that was divided by a huge black rubber sheet. The sheet was glistening with oil. When we went behind it, it was pitch black and crowded with people. We rubbed against people in the dark. Everyone was just sliding and slipping off each other with all the oil. It was weird but exciting.

There were other rooms covered in mattresses that were a mass of writhing limbs. It was great to watch. It was a bit like being at an old-fashioned carnival. The people were old and young, able-bodied and disabled, beautiful and ugly. There was a strong smell of rubber, oil

"Quite a few people had black, rubber masks on."

incense, and sweat, and it all combined to make a very heady
atmosphere. I found it incredibly arousing. Because everyone
around me was losing their inhibitions, I found it quite easy to
lose mine too.

My boyfriend and I met a girl who teased us with her whip and asked
us if we wanted to use it on her. We ended up spending most of the
night with her. The three of us had a wonderful time – we touched,
flirted, and teased each other. I did things I never imagined I would.
The whole experience was pretty intense."

If you visit any of the festivals or exhibitions of erotica that are held in major Western cities, you will be confronted with dozens of people who make it their job to parade themselves sexually. The costumes of these erotic performance artists are exotic and mostly minimal. You can see women dressed in basques, high heels, thongs, nipple tassles, catsuits, angel wings, and rubber dresses. You can see men dressed in chains, dog collars, masks, skimpy uniforms, and body paint... the variety is endless. For those of us who enjoy looking, the people who dress up and parade are a major part of the show's attraction.

Parading and spectating

You can bring some exhibitionism into your sex life by deliberately dressing up and parading for your lover. You can also be an exhibitionist in other ways, for example, doing household jobs naked in front of your lover (or wearing kinky underwear), surprising your lover by wearing something new or unusual in bed, or stripping for them (see pages 124–127). Exhibitionism is especially exciting when it's not expected.

Party trick

Next time you go to a party, or you throw one yourself, make a point of dressing down. Halfway through the evening, when the party's in full swing, tell your lover you're going to disappear for a while. Sneak into the bathroom and swap your everyday outfit for something exotic and glamorous, such as crimson lipstick, heels, and a black PVC dress, or – for men – leather trousers and a harness top. If you can, recruit an accomplice who can help you get dressed, and who can then announce your "arrival" to the party. When you've got everyone's attention, make a sexy entrance by going directly to your lover and delivering a long and passionate kiss.

Wear an apron – and nothing else.

Dinner date

Invite your lover to dinner (even if you live together). Light some candles and ask your lover to wait patiently for the food to be served. Re-appear some minutes later bearing the starter – and dressed in the kinkiest outfit you can get hold of. For example, a rubber apron – and nothing else – for men (even kinkier if there's a hole at crotch level!), or nipple clamps and a sarong for women. The rule is that your lover has to look but not touch for the duration of the meal. When the main course is finished, you can climb onto the table and cheekily announce that you're the next thing to be eaten.

You can make just as much of a style statement with your pubic hair as you can with the hair on your head. Trim it, shave it, wax it, dye it, or decorate it – the choice is yours.

Hot hair styles

The Brazilian, the Playboy, and the Hollywood

These are for those who prefer no hair down there, or just the tiniest strip of hair. The Brazilian is a pubic hair style that involves waxing everything except a rectangle – nicknamed a landing strip – at the front. Gwyneth Paltrow famously claimed that it changed her life. This style is named after Brazilian women who waxed their pubes in order to wear tiny thongs on the beach. More dramatic than a Brazilian is a Hollywood, in which all pubic hair is removed – some women say being "bare" enhances sexual sensation. In between a Brazilian and a Hollywood is a Playboy – just a tiny line of hair at the front.

Tailor-made styles

Surprise your lover: decorate your pubic area with flowers, stickers, or crystals (check these out on the internet). Or wax it into an interesting shape. You can buy waxing stencils in the shape of hearts, stars, arrows, lightning bolts, and Xs. You can also dye your pubes exotic colours. The "Tiffany Box" style describes pubic hair that's dyed blue and waxed into a square shape.

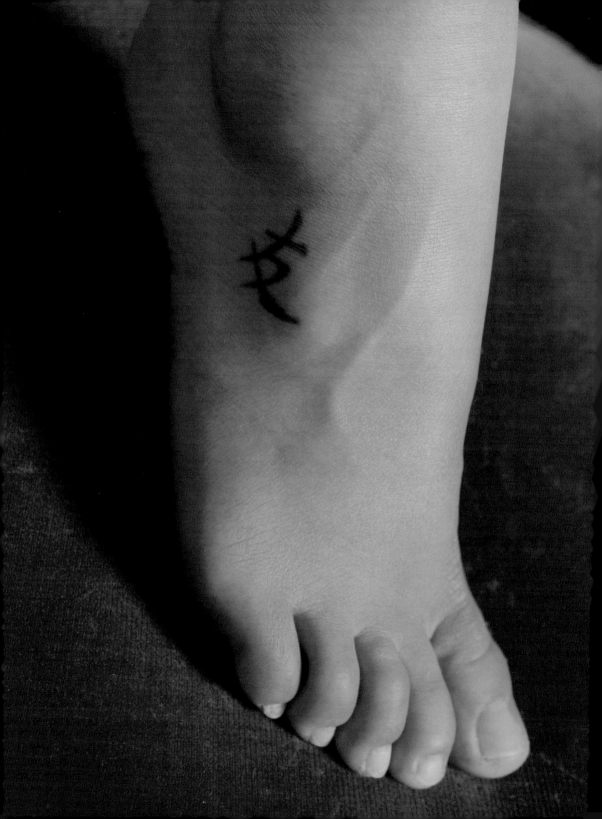

Tattoos don't have to be permanent. You can buy temporary tattoo ink that lasts for about three days. Drawing your own design on your lover is a unique erotic ritual – a secret that only the two of you know about.

Tattoo or not to

Choose a favourite erogenous zone on your lover's body and get drawing. Alternatively, give yourself a tattoo and then surprise your lover by revealing it in bed. Good sites for a sexy tattoo are the navel, the pubic area (if it's waxed), the breasts, the inner thighs, and the buttocks. Here are some tattoo concepts.

◆ Romantic tattoos: draw hearts or a ring of flowers around the navel. Alternatively, write your names.
◆ Kinky tattoos: draw an arrow from your navel pointing down to your genitals. Draw lips and a tongue near your lover's nipples or genitals.
◆ Message tattoos: write a word or a message such as: "Flirt!", or "I want you!", "Lick here!", or "Stroke me!".
◆ Abstract tattoos: draw your own pattern, or copy a Celtic design (there are plenty to be found on the internet).

A word of warning: if you fancy having a permanent tattoo, think about it for at least three days before going ahead.

Games and fantasies

Vanilla sex is the term for straight, unkinky sex. It's a great experience, but there are also times when you might want to be more adventurous. Role-playing games, experimenting with props, and enacting sexual fantasies are all wonderful ways to make sex naughty, creative, and playful.

Are you a game player?

TAKE OUR QUIZ AND FIND OUT... IF YOU DARE

Some people are naturally reserved in bed; others love to fantasize, play, and explore. Answer the following questions with your lover to find out which category you fall into.

1 When you have a sexual fantasy, what do you do?

a. Keep it to yourselves.
b. Describe it to each other.
c. Act it out together.

2 Which of these best describes your sex life?

a. We tend to always have sex in the same way.
b. We experiment when we're in the mood.
c. We're always trying out new positions, sex toys, and kinky games.

3 Who goes on top?

a. Always me, or always my lover.
b. Either of us.
c. A third person.

4 Do you dress up for sex?

a. No, we take our clothes off.
b. Occasionally.
c. Doesn't everyone?

5 Have you ever used restraints?

a. No, we don't see the point.
b. A few times.
c. Yes, we love power games.

MOSTLY As You're quite straight sexually. If you want to extend your boundaries, read the next four chapters – preferably in bed together.
MOSTLY Bs You're explorers – when you want to be. Read on.
MOSTLY Cs There's no doubt that you're sexual adventurers. I hope this book gives you lots of ideas and inspiration.

Play by the rules

When you play sex games with your lover, you need to trust each other and feel safe in the knowledge that your lover isn't going to laugh or criticise you. It's also useful to have some ground rules to prevent things getting out of hand. For example, if you are embarrassed, anxious, or in physical discomfort, you need to know that you can end the game.

Shouting the word "stop" isn't necessarily the best way to end a game because people often say this as a way of heightening eroticism during role play. This is why I suggest using a code word instead. A code word can be anything you like, as long as it can't be misconstrued.

The ground rules

◆ Agree a code word and honour it.

◆ Tell your lover if there are activities that you don't want to try.

◆ Promise your lover that what you do together will remain absolutely private. Never exhibit photographs or other personal details about your lover in public, on the internet, or on your mobile phone.

◆ Don't introduce a third person into your sex play without prior discussion and mutual agreement. Don't hurt or mark your lover.

Spanking raises sexual tension in two ways. Firstly, it gives a novel physical sensation – it makes the skin feel hot and tingly. Secondly, spanking offers a psychological thrill. The message it sends is: "I'm in charge and I want you to know it". Psychologists say that we often get off on feeling powerful or dominated.

Sexy spanking

You can include spanking in your usual foreplay or intercourse, but if it's the psychological thrill that you're after, role play is the best way of ramping up the sexual charge. Choose roles that are obviously dominant and submissive, such as headmaster and naughty student.

Spanking tips

◆ If you are the spankee, bend across your lover's knees or get on all fours. The vulnerability of such poses is a big part of the eroticism.

◆ Good spanking positions during sex are the doggie position and a straightforward man- or woman-on-top position.

◆ Spank by clapping the palm of the hand on the fleshy part of the buttock (or use a specially-designed paddle). Do not spank on bone.

◆ After a spank, rub your partner's buttocks and sympathise.

◆ Spanking should be fun and erotic. Stop spanking if your partner says the code word (see page 54).

Kinky games

You and your lover are feeling amorous and you fancy doing something just a little bit different. Luckily, the props you need are things that you might just find in your kitchen or bathroom cupboard.

Tantalize your lover by rubbing your body over theirs.

All wrapped up

Ask your lover to strip. When they've done so, put a blindfold on them and tell them that you're going to "dress" them. Get a roll of plastic film and wind it around your lover's body – wind it tight around the chest or breasts, buttocks, and genitals so you have the thrill of seeing these parts tightly encased in transparent film. If you want to, you can use plastic film as a restraining device to bind your lover's arms and legs.

Remove your lover's blindfold and let them see what you've done. Now tantalize your lover by rubbing your body over their's. Stimulate their nipples and genitals through the film. To make love, make a "sex-sized" hole in the film. Warning: don't put plastic film on your lover's face.

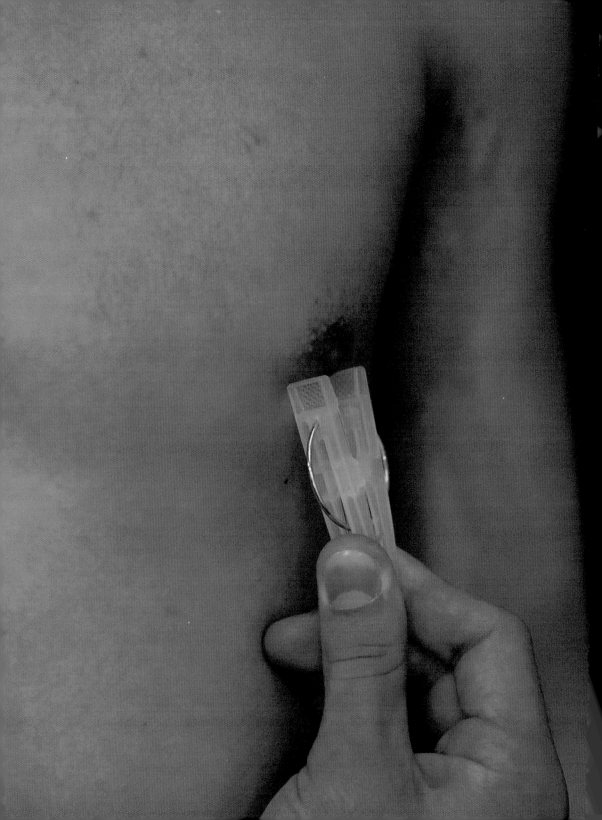

Sweet love

If you've got a sweet tooth, bring the thrill of the candy store home to the bedroom. Treat your lover to a series of sweet sex tricks: hide a mint lozenge in your mouth as you kiss them; tie some liquorice lace loosely around his penis and then eat it; demonstrate fellatio on a lollipop; give oral sex with a mouthful of popping sherbet; or arrange a candy trail along your body ending in the place you want to be licked, sucked, or kissed.

*Tell them how dirty they are.
Lead them to the bathroom.*

Discipline techniques

If you like games of dominance and submission (see pages 68–71), try popping a pair of black rubber gloves on your hands and asking your lover to lie down. It's inspection time! Take your time to look carefully at your lover's body for dirt. Tell them how dirty they are, then lead them to the bathroom where you will give them a good wash – pay close attention to the "dirty" bits.

Afterwards, use household objects to inflict mild discomfort on your lover. Have you ever noticed those tiny clothes pegs used for hanging greetings cards? Here's a different use for them: put them on your lover's nipples. Or use a fly swat for some light spanking (see page 56),

Rubber games

Some of the sexiest garments I've ever seen have been
made of rubber. Oiled to a high gloss with their occupants
apparently poured inside, all you want to do is slide around
their incredible curves. When you dress up in rubber, make
sure that you use a specially designed rubber gloss to make
your assets shine.

Fetish nurse

Slide into in a rubber dress and tell your lover that you need to give
them a medical examination. Ask them to lie down. Your job is to
check that their genitals are functioning well. Don't reveal any signs
that you're aroused yourself – your role is purely professional. Later
on you can lie down and wait for your patient to express their thanks.

Zipper sex

Lots of rubber costumes have strategically placed zippers for access to
erotic zones. Unzip these one at a time and stimulate the exposed areas
for a minute each. When your lover is turned on, tell them that you're
going unzip their crotch area and time how long they take to climax.
Tell your lover that if they haven't come within a specified period, the
zipper will be done up. But be prepared to make love a little later!

Good games

I've called these good games because they are creative
games that engage the imagination and give you both a
sense of playful enjoyment. If you want to explore the
darker side of sex, try the naughty games on pages 68–71.

*Describe very precisely what you
are going to do to your lover.*

Sex out loud

It's often said that the most important sex organ is the brain. It's true.
Titillating your lover with erotic ideas and suggestions is a powerful
means of seduction. The secret is to describe in very precise detail
exactly what you are going to do to your lover. For example, tell him
that you're going to kiss him along the length of his spine, then you're
going to turn him turn over so that you can kiss and stroke his penis
and balls. Finally, you're going to climb on top and slide yourself onto
his erect penis.

The sexiest way to deliver these kinds of suggestions is by whispering
in your lover's ear. When you've completed your description, make
sure you deliver what you have promised.

The lost valley

In this game, one of you takes the role of the explorer while the other takes the role of a naked tribesperson. If you are the explorer, imagine that you have landed on a uncharted island. After travelling deep into the interior through the jungle, you eventually come across a tribe that appears to know nothing about sex. Your job is to sensitively instruct a selected tribesperson about how sex should be done. You take advantage of the situation by requesting that your favourite techniques are tried out on you. If you are playing the role of the tribesperson, you are not only keen and curious to learn about sex, you are completely free from any inhibition or sense of shyness.

Go to work on your subject using hand, mouth, or sex toy.

The sex scientist

One of you plays the role of a sex scientist and the other plays the role of a laboratory subject. The sex scientist's job is to find out how many orgasms one person can have in a single day. Go to work on your subject by hand, mouth, or using any appropriate sex toy such as a vibrator, dildo, or anal beads (or all of them). Many people stop at one orgasm, but some go on to have three or four or more – very exceptionally, and usually when very young, they can manage more. (One Hungarian friend said he had sex 16 times, but then he was aged 16 at the time!)

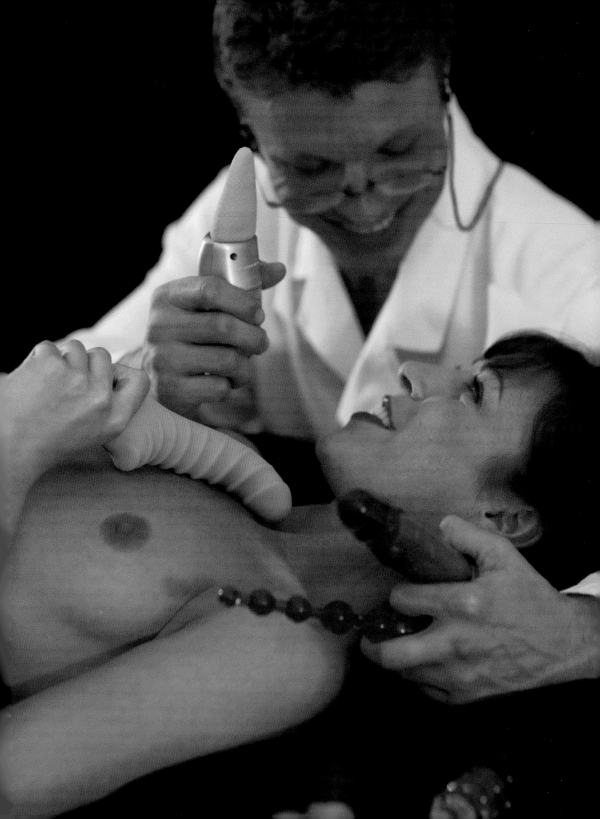

Naughty games are so-called because they explore the darker side of sex, otherwise known as "BDSM". This stands for "bondage, domination, submission, and masochism". Decide which of you is going to be the "dom" and which of you the "sub". As the dom you must dress powerfully. If you are the sub, all you need are a few leather straps or chains strategically placed. Now act out one of these scenarios.

Naughty games

Fantasy scenarios

◆ You are a dungeon master/mistress and your lover is your victim.

◆ You own a grand house and your lover is your youngest servant.

◆ You are the headteacher and your lover is an errant pupil.

◆ You are the prison governor and your lover is the prisoner.

The aim is for the dom to punish the sub by, for example, inflicting mild discomfort or humiliation, restraining movement, or giving and then withdrawing sexual stimulation. Handcuffs, whips, chains, canes, straps, cords, and blindfolds are all useful props for the dom.

How to be a good dom

- Tell your lover exactly what you want them to do. Don't say "please" or "thank you."
- Speak in a different voice from usual if that makes it easier for you to get into character.
- Punish your lover if they dare to disobey your commands.
- Alternatively, be a wicked dom by making your punishment unpredictable. Lull your victim into a false sense of security by being loving and caressing and then punish them again for no good reason.
- Decorate the room – pitch black for a dungeon, for example.

Lull your victim into a false
sense of security by being
loving and caressing.

How to be a good sub

- Behave in a completely servile way.
- Speak in an obedient way, such as: "yes master/mistress".
- Use subservient body language, such as kneeling, being on all fours, and always looking up at your lover.
- Play up your role by saying "thank you" or expressing gratitude for punishment.
- Agree on a code word (see page 84). You may even want to have two code words: the first means "let's cool things down a bit". The second means: "let's stop straight away".

Room service

"I made a great show of bending over to plump up the pillows."

"I got there early and dressed in a super-skimpy chambermaid outfit. We had agreed to stay in role right from the beginning so I let my lover into the room and explained that I was still fixing his bed, but he was more than welcome to sit down and wait until I had finished. I showed him a bottle of champagne chilling in the fridge and told him that he could pour it out if he wanted to.

When I knew my lover was watching, I made a great show of bending over to plump up the pillows and shake up the duvet. I was just wearing a tiny thong under my uniform.

My lover sat there watching me with obvious amusement and enjoyment – I could see his erection through his trousers. I said he was looking tired, and I asked him if he wanted me to help him off with his jacket.

Of course, I took off more than his jacket and he ended up naked. Without batting an eyelid I offered to help him into bed and then I let my uniform slip off and I climbed on top of him. He asked me if this was all part of the room service and I said 'yes'.

I kissed him on the mouth and then I very slowly moved down his body flicking my tongue over his chest and belly. Then I gave him a very slow and sensual blow job. He loved it and came quickly. By this point I was incredibly turned on but, to stay in character, I made myself get off him and pretend to leave.

"To stay in character I made myself get off him and pretend to leave."

Just as I got to the door he asked me to stop. I went as nonchalantly as I could back to the bed. He took off my bra and G-string and started to caress me. He kissed and licked my breasts and then he made me climax by hand.

It was an exciting experience, mainly because we both stayed in character and because we were in a completely different place from usual. It was pure escapism and it'll be something we'll talk about for ages. Afterwards, we got under the duvet and drank the champagne together."

Erotic treats

3

To keep sex playful, exciting, and naughty I recommend
that you give yourself and your lover plenty of erotic treats,
such as sexy phone calls and saucy presents. Massage is also
a wonderful gift to receive. In this chapter, you'll find several
different types of massage from oil wrestling to Tantric
massage. You can even massage your lover using just
your teeth! I've also included a couple of erotic
treats for you to do on your own.

Sex profile

 EROTIC INTERVIEW

Do you really know what your lover finds erotic? Here are some questions to help you find out. You might just uncover a secret desire.

1 What's your idea of sexual bliss – fast, passionate sex on the kitchen counter or taking turns to give each other an erotic massage that lasts all afternoon?

2 Would you prefer me to wake you up with sex in the morning or seduce you last thing at night before we go to sleep?

3 How would you most like me to touch your genitals?

4 Do you get turned on by mild pain?

5 How much kissing, caressing, and stroking do you like before we have sex?

6 What's your favourite sexual fantasy? Can we act it out?

7 What are your top three erogenous zones (apart from the clitoris and penis)?

8 How would you most like me to touch you in these erogenous zones? Do you enjoy a light caress or firm pressure? Or do you like a mixture of both?

If these questions lead to more questions, go ahead and ask them. Imagine that you've never had sex with your lover before and it's your job to build up a really detailed picture of their sexual tastes. Now swap roles. It's your lover's turn to put these questions to you.

Bites and nibbles

Bites and nibbles make your lover's flesh shiver and tingle with pleasure. The secret of biting is to know which parts of the body respond best. Good parts of the body to bite or nibble include the neck, shoulders, ears, the tops of the arms, the buttocks, the fleshy areas of the hands, and the tops of the thighs. Avoid biting bony areas.

Whichever part of your lover's body you bite, be aware of their pain threshold – most people enjoy playful bites in which the teeth caress or graze the skin, rather than bear down upon it. If your lover is nervous, tell them that you are going to massage – rather than bite – them with your tongue, lips, and teeth, and that you'll be gentle.

Intimate bites

If you want to try biting your lover's penis, make sure it is really well lubricated with saliva (or any other lubricant) and let your teeth glide gently up and down on the shaft. Apply minimal pressure with your teeth – if you want to apply more pressure, ask your lover for guidance about what feels acceptable. Biting the clitoris and labia demands the same caution. Start by sucking the labia or clitoris and then bring your teeth softly onto their surface, then try daisy nibbles (see page 83). Don't go any further without your lover's permission.

Sucking bites

Draw up the flesh into your mouth and secure it with your teeth. Now suck hard – imagine you're a vampire. This produces the classic red mark of the love bite. Ask first if you want to bite a part of your lover that is on show!

Pulling bites

Gently take part of your lover's body between your teeth. Apply just enough pressure with your teeth to hold onto their flesh. Now move your head away very slowly so that your lover's flesh gets gently pulled through your teeth. This should stimulate rather than cause pain.

Sound bites

As you nibble and bite your way along your lover's body, press your lips against their skin and make a soft humming sound as you exhale. The vibrations will feel tantalizing.

Daisy nibbles

This is the gentlest type of bite imaginable. You can practice it on the tip of your lover's little finger. Part your teeth very slightly (enough to allow a drinking straw into your mouth) and rest them on your lover's skin. Now very slowly and gently bring your teeth together so that your teeth slide over the surface without trapping or nipping the skin. Do this repeatedly.

There are times when everyone's sex life can benefit from a little expert intervention. These are six suggestions that I've drawn from sex therapy – they can help women reach orgasm, help men last longer, and generally add that extra frisson of pleasure to your sex life.

Expert attention - six special sex tips

The Grind: this is a wonderful sex position for women because the base of the penis moves directly against the clitoris. Many other sex positions don't involve direct clitoral stimulation, so it can sometimes be tricky for women to climax without extra help. The Grind is also an exciting position for men because it produces novel sensations on the penis.

To do the Grind the woman lies on her back and the man gets on top. Both of you have your legs straight. Once he's inside her, he moves his body as high up hers as he can (to bring the base of his penis into maximum contact with her clitoris). Then instead of thrusting in and out, the man wriggles and grinds in a side-to-side movement. This ensures lots of wonderful pressure on her clitoris.

2 Make an agreement not to have sex for a week. Instead, spend time in bed just touching, massaging, and stroking each other. Rediscover what feels good. Talk to each other in detail about how you like to be touched on different parts of your body.

3 This is a technique to help men last longer by delaying ejaculation. Men: when you feel you're close to coming, grasp your testicles and pull them gently but firmly downward. It's worth practising this during masturbation before you try it during sex.

4 Surprise your lover by spontaneously seducing them in the middle of the day. Make it so spontaneous that she just sits on his lap without bothering to take her clothes off, for example.

5 Experiment with condoms. Make it into a game by pretending you're professional condom testers. Rate a whole range of them in terms of aesthetics, fun and novelty, and sensation. Try textured ones, micro-thin ones, flavoured ones, and shaped ones. There's even a condom that heats up on body contact.

6 Light some candles and put some cushions and throws on the floor of your room. Sit naked in front of a mirror together and describe everything you love about each other's body. This is a great way to feel more confident about your body. Always emphasize the positive – never be critical of your lover's appearance. Now take it in turns to give each other slow and sensual oral sex in front of the mirror.

Oil wrestling

There is a whole sexual movement devoted to getting
oiled up and wrestling and slipping around on each other.
You can do it in groups at fetish clubs or by yourselves at
home. The thrill comes from getting totally messy and
abandoning all control.

To get slippery at home you first need to oil-proof your bed or floor.
You can use an old shower curtain for this or – if you're really into
slippery oil games – you can buy a PVC fitted bedsheet in a sexy
colour such as black, red, or pink.

To lubricate each other's naked body you can use any kind of oil
you like: baby oil, massage oil, or olive oil. You can also use other
substances such as cream, honey, or syrup but the effect is more
sticky and less slippery. The only other prop you'll need is a timer.

Now comes the fun bit: lie down together on your protective sheet, set
the timer for two minutes, and start wriggling and wrestling. Imagine
you're a couple of slippery seals writhing and undulating in all
directions. The aim is to get your lover on their back and slide across
their body. Whoever does this first is the winner and gets to demand
a sexual favour! Warning: don't use and oil and condoms together.

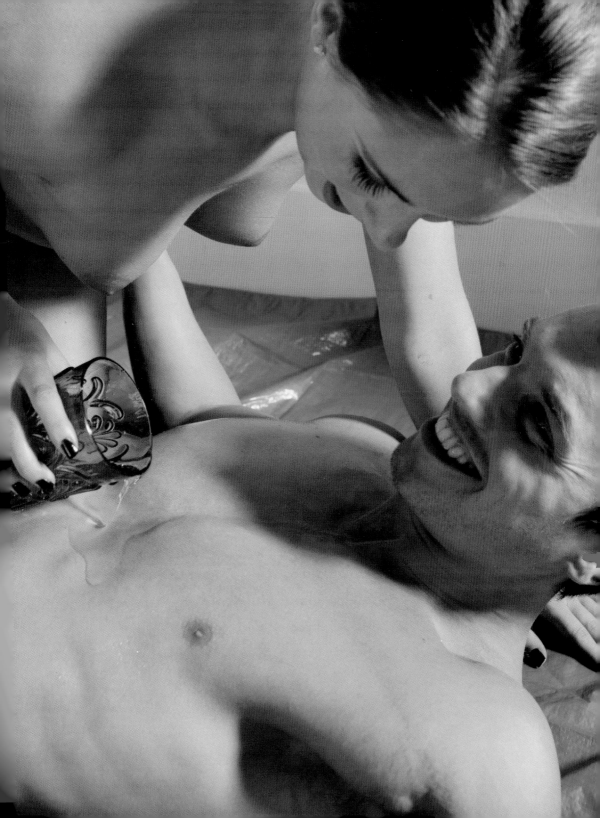

Hot massage

People often fantasize about a sexual encounter in which
they simply lie back and have all their desires met. Instead
of reciprocating, their only job is to drift off into a world
of erotic pleasure. When you've got plenty of time, lead
your lover into the bedroom, ask them
to lie down, and tell them to
close their eyes – the x-rated
massage is about to begin.

Hot massage for him

Cover the front of his body with oil. Start by massaging the front of his body (including his penis), first with a firm stroke and then with a light stroke. The firm stroke will relax him, whereas the light stroke will make him shiver with erotic pleasure. Use just your fingertips or fingernails to barely graze the surface of his skin.

Halfway through your massage, slowly crawl across your lover until you are straddling his abdomen. Imagine that your vagina is an extra massage hand and manoeuvre your vagina so that it slides over his penis. Every time you massage his chest, rise and fall on his penis. Don't think of your pleasure – just focus on his. If he doesn't climax like this, continue by giving his penis a firm hand massage.

Hot massage for her

Coat your hands in oil and massage her breasts. Slide your hands in diagonal lines from below each breast to the shoulder on the opposite side of her body. Then concentrate on her nipples – move your palms in circles on top of them and then tweak them with your fingers.

Move your hands to your lover's genitals. Use one hand in slow, gentle circles on her clitoris and your other hand to apply static pressure to her G-spot (on the front wall of her vagina). Watch her responses and move your hand faster on her clitoris as she becomes more aroused. Slowly guide a second or third finger into her vagina and move them slowly in and out caressing the front vaginal wall as you go.

You don't have to wait for Valentine's day to give your lover an erotic gift. A surprise present at any time of the year is a great way to make your lover feel desired and sexy. Be creative in the way that you deliver your gifts. For example, exotic fruit is a gift that is just waiting to be eaten directly from your body and a bunch of red roses (thornless ones) is an innovative spanking tool!

Valentine treats

Erotic vouchers

These are gift tokens with a sexy twist – each one can be redeemed for the erotic favour it describes. Examples of erotic favours include specific acts such as oral sex, anal sex, or a G-spot massage. They can also promise things such as: "you get to choose when we have sex for the next week", or "sex in the position of your choice for the next five times we make love". If your voucher describes a sexual act, go into explicit detail in the "fine print". Use your most lascivious writing skills.

Pillow gifts

If you're going away from your lover for a while, leave them something extra special underneath their pillow. Suggestions include: a penis-head stimulator for him; a vibrator that she can attach to her finger; or a toy duck that vibrates in the bath (for either of you).

Tantric massage aims to build up arousal slowly so that men stay near the peak of arousal for as long as possible without ejaculating. This means that he is able to experience intense sexual pleasure for much longer than he usually would. The trick is to get very close to ejaculation but not to surrender to it – this is sometimes referred to in Tantra as "riding the wave".

Tantricks – sex touch for him

Women: you need plenty of oil to give your lover a Tantric massage (but remember that oil damages latex condoms). Start by giving him an all-over body massage to make him feel relaxed and receptive. Explain that the genital massage you're about to give is not intended to make him ejaculate. Ask him to tell you if he feels he is close to coming.

Begin by stroking your lover's penis in long, slow, firm strokes. Next, do the up-and-down stroke, which consists of holding his penis at the base with your right hand, sliding your hand up and off, then quickly following with your left hand. Then change direction so that you start the movement at the top of the penis and slide down.

The next stroke is the "juicer", which consists of swivelling the palm and fingers of your hand over the head of the penis as if you were juicing an orange. If your lover tells you that he is close to coming at any stage, move the site of your massage to his abdomen or chest for a while. If he is about to ejaculate, grasp his balls and pull them gently but firmly downward.

There is a spot, known in Tantra as the sacred spot, which lies halfway along his perineum.

Next, stroke and massage his testicles using plenty of oil. Work your way along his perineum (the area between his testicles and his anus). There is a spot, known in Tantra as the sacred spot, which lies halfway along his perineum. It yields intensely erotic feelings; you may feel it as a small indentation. Apply firm, static pressure to the sacred spot (or move your fingers in tiny circles) and ask your lover how it feels. You may need to explore and experiment before you find the right place and pressure.

Finally, massage his penis with one hand and press his sacred spot with the other. Prolong the massage for as long as you can. Your aim is to keep him near the brink of orgasm, but not to push him over the edge.

As with Tantric massage for men, Tantric touch for women should start with whole-body strokes. Touch your lover's genitals only when her whole body is humming with sensuality. Tell your lover that the aim of the massage is not to make her reach orgasm, but to create a build up of sexual energy that she can relax into and enjoy.

Tantricks – sex touch for her

When you're massaging her body you can enhance the sensations she receives by strapping a vibrating massager to your hand. Alternatively, massage her with a scratchy bath mitt filled with oil. The oil seeps out onto her skin and the sensations she experiences are a delicious combination of smooth and rough.

Start your genital massage by gently stroking and squeezing her pubic mound and labia. Make sure your hands are really well lubricated with oil – you can discard the scratchy mitt for this bit! Take her labia between your thumb and index finger and gently pull them. Explore the inner part of her vulva with your fingertips – move them in clockwise and anticlockwise circles around her clitoris (keep everything slow) and then down towards her vaginal entrance

Stroke around her vaginal entrance and then slowly insert one or more fingers into her vagina. Try to breathe in time with each other – make your breaths slow and deep so that they go right down to your belly. Breathing in synchrony helps to connect you and it keeps you both centred and relaxed. Make your fingers straight and stiff and move them slowly in and out of her vagina stroking the vaginal walls with the pads of your fingers as you go. You can use your other hand to stroke her clitoris. If your lover gets close to orgasm at any point, stop stimulating her vagina and clitoris until she becomes slightly less aroused – try stroking her belly for a while instead.

G-spot massage

With your fingers in her vagina, crook them in such a way that the pads of your fingers press against the front wall of her vagina. Explore this sensitive area by pressing, circling, and sliding your fingertips. Finally, apply static pressure to her G-spot, an area that protrudes from the vaginal wall (if this is difficult to find, ask your lover for guidance about which area is most sensitive). While you are touching your lover's G-spot, you can also insert a finger from your other hand into her anus. Ask first whether this is acceptable, and don't use this finger to touch her genitals afterwards.

Explore her vagina by pressing, circling, and sliding your fingertips.

Tantric sexercises

The sexually sophisticated have been quick to realise the value of ancient Tantric teaching. Tantric sex exercises emphasize the value of slowness, the importance of whole-body eroticism, and the spirituality of sexual ecstasy. Tantric sex books and workshops are widely available and you can spend a weekend, or longer, going back to Tantric sex basics. Here's my mini Tantric course. It lasts from Friday to Sunday.

Day 1 (Friday)

Spend time going for walks together, ideally in a beautiful or tranquil place. Talk and relax. Get to know each other better. Reconnect. Spend some time making your bedroom into a haven. Get rid of clutter. Make the lighting soft – or light candles – and drape your bed in sensuous throws or fabrics.

At the end of the day, sit cross-legged and look deeply into each other's eyes (this is called soul-gazing). Hold each other's gaze for several minutes. Breathe in synchrony with each other. After a while, hug each other. Let your whole body melt into the embrace. Stay here for as long as you like. Go to bed with each other, but don't have sex – just enjoy the mood of warmth and intimacy.

Day 2 (Saturday)

Spend Saturday morning lightly stroking and caressing one another's naked bodies (but not having intercourse). Eat a light lunch, then repeat the stroking in the afternoon. This time, imagine that every touch you bestow upon your lover can be felt by you. Talk about any emotions that come up during this exercise. Listen to whatever your lover says to you without judgement or criticism. Finish the day with the soul-gazing exercise (see day 1) and a long, melting hug. Imagine that you are merging your sense of identity with that of your lover's so that the boundaries between the two of you start to dissolve.

Have sex in which he thrusts slowly and gently.

Day 3 (Sunday)

On Sunday morning, stroke each other all over and then concentrate on arousing each other (try the Tantric touch for him and her on pages 96–103) and then move on to intercourse. (Men: rather than thrusting inside your lover, penetrate her and be still. Enjoy the sensuality of being inside her and wait until your erection subsides.) In the afternoon, repeat the morning's exercise, then have intercourse in which he thrusts slowly and gently. Breathe in synchrony. If you reach orgasm, fine, but if you don't, that's fine too. The emphasis should be on the connection between the two of you. End the day with soul-gazing (see day 1) and talk about what you have discovered over the weekend.

Tantric workshop

HOW WAS IT FOR YOU

"We concentrated on drawing sexual energy up inside our bodies."

"We spent the first day of the course doing simple exercises that were designed to get us in touch our partners – literally. There were lots of stroking and massage exercises. The teacher also explained how instead of racing to have an orgasm during sex we could hold onto sexual energy. She said this would help sex to become slower, more erotic, and more sensual. She taught us some breathing exercises in which we concentrated on drawing up sexual energy inside our bodies. We did most of the exercises in the same room as the other couples, but if there was anything explicitly sexual, we had to go back to our own room to try it. We reported back to the teacher afterwards.

On the next day of the course we did an exercise that was simple, but really amazing. We had sex without moving. He was inside me and we just concentrated on our breathing. I kept him hard by contracting my vaginal muscles.

We both had to imagine erotic feelings rising up within our bodies as we inhaled. The effect was wonderful. It was like nothing else existed apart from my lover inside me, and the two of us breathing in and out. Breathing felt incredibly blissful. And all of the usual distracting thoughts that go through my head during sex weren't there anymore. I had a lovely warm, tingling feeling.

As a result of the course we've learned to be more sensual and connected in our everyday life. Sex isn't just about having an orgasm. We take things much more slowly. Sometimes we can spend a couple

"Nothing else existed apart from my lover inside me."

of hours making love. And if we start to have sex and then we stop, it doesn't matter in the way that it might have done once. We're much more accepting of each other, and sex feels more intimate and loving than it used to.

When you can be really open with your lover, you feel incredibly warm towards each other. And we've learned to talk to each other about our feelings more than we used to. I met one couple at the workshop who told me that it made them closer – and improved their sex life – after 27 years of marriage."

Whether your lover lives in a different continent or the
same house, phone sex can be a great part of your sexual
repertoire. It is a wonderfully naughty and exciting way to
stay in touch with each other.

Phone sex

Ten ways to give good phone sex

1 Give yourself open-ended time. Phone sex doesn't work very well if you
have only five minutes. It also helps to arrange a specific time for phone
sex, so that you can enjoy the anticipation and make sure you are in a
place that is private and relaxing.

2 Start with small talk, such as how your day has been. Build up to
eroticism gradually by asking, for example, "what are you wearing?"

3 It's natural to feel shy at first, but closing your eyes and imagining your
lover is right there beside you can go a long way to help.

4 Tell your lover exactly what you want to do to them or what you want
them to do to you. Be explicit and specific in your descriptions. The
more detail you go into the better.

5 If you feel inhibited and don't know what to say, role play can help. Try pretending that you're strangers. Imagine, for example, that the "stranger" has called a wrong number, but you carry on talking anyway. Tell them they have a sexy voice. Ask them if they are on their own. Play coy by, for example, asking for the stranger's permission to touch yourself while you're on the phone.

6 As you become more aroused describe to your lover the way in which you're touching yourself and how good it feels.

7 If you know your lover has a particular fantasy or fetish make sure you incorporate it in the dialogue.

8 Make as much noise as you want to. Sound effects are important. Breathe, moan, pant – your lover needs to hear you in order to get to the peak of arousal.

9 Tell your lover when you're close to coming as this can take their arousal levels up to the next level.

10 If you come first, keep "stimulating" your lover by making sounds and talking. After orgasm, spend some time "coming down" by talking intimately. You can also ask your lover if the two of you can just be silent at the end of the line and listen to each other's breathing – do whatever works best to create that mood of post-sex intimacy. Don't put the phone down until both of you feel ready.

Next time you're feeling sexy and you have some privacy, try this naked self-touch. Lie or sit in a comfortable position. Rather than touching your penis straight away, try touching other areas, other erogenous zones, that you like: your nipples, your belly, the inside of your thighs.

Self-touch – him

Now imagine a beautiful woman is touching your penis. How would she touch it? Would she let the fingertips play on your scrotum before reaching for your erection? Would she manipulate your foreskin? Would she rub your penis hard and fast, or slowly and softly? Would she caress the place between your balls and anus? Embellish the fantasy in your mind as much as possible before you start touching yourself. Let your mind freewheel – you're not in any rush.

When you take your penis in your hand, touch it in the way that you've been imagining, rather than the habitual way in which you masturbate. Even if it doesn't feel natural at first, keep going, and picture your fantasy woman in your touch. Tease yourself by getting close to ejaculation and then stopping. Do this three or four times before finally allowing yourself to come.

Close the door to your bedroom and enjoy some private time by yourself. There's nothing like some sexual self-discovery to improve your sex life. After all, if you know what sort of touch you really like, you can give your man direct instructions.

Self-touch — her

Equip the bedroom and bathroom as if for a lovers' encounter. You will be making love – to yourself. Have a hot, scented, candlelit bath. Afterwards, lie back on a mound of cushions and towels. Let some oil trickle into the palm of your hand and then rub it into your neck, shoulders, breasts, and belly. Sink into the sensuality of the moment.

Now use your oiled hands to caress your genitals. Don't touch your clitoris at first – instead use both hands to explore. Let your fingertips press, glide, and slide. Note which areas are sensitive and which are not. Dip your fingers into your vagina and press on the parts that feel most sensitive. Move your finger up to your clitoris and see if you prefer circling on the clitoral head itself, or around it, or on either side. Build on the good sensations. If you are about to climax, change the speed or the rhythm. Keep yourself near climax for about 15 minutes

Pushing back the boundaries

4

Memorable sex tends to be unusual sex which takes you out of your comfort zone. For some people, stripping or having sex outdoors feels risqué; for others, threesomes or hiring a lover for the night is the meaning of experimental. Whatever your boundaries, push them back by trying something different.

How far will you go?

TAKE OUR QUIZ AND FIND OUT... IF YOU DARE

Where do your sexual boundaries lie? How far will you push them or let them be pushed? Answer the following questions to find out.

1 You want to do something new with your lover. Which of these is most likely?

a. Sex in a different position.
b. Sex in the garden.
c. Sex in a threesome.

2 A party you're at is turning into an orgy. What do you do?

a. Get your coat and leave.
b. Watch. You're nervous yet excited.
c. Strip off and throw yourself into the action.

3 Your lover wants you to dance for them. What do you do?

a. Dance with your clothes on.
b. Dance naked.
c. Strip provocatively and dance dirtily.

4 What's the sexiest thing you could film with a movie camera?

a. My lover getting undressed.
b. Us having sex.
c. Us having group sex.

MOSTLY As You're not keen on novelty in your sex life. If you want to change this, there are plenty of ideas in this chapter.

MOSTLY Bs You find sexual naughtiness and adventure enticing. Talk to your lover about taking things further.

MOSTLY Cs You are pretty open and exhibitionist when it comes to sex. Enjoy it but don't always put yourself under pressure to perform.

Strip for me!

Stripping is an extremely sexy gift to a lover. It's also a great way to boost your sexual confidence. Traditionally, women have stripped for men, but there's no reason why men can't perform for women too. When you strip, tell your lover in advance that it's alright to look, but not to touch. Your aim, above all, is to tease.

If you've never stripped before, it's normal to feel self-conscious. The best tips for the inexperienced stripper are: practice and prepare. Get your costume together in advance, practice your stripping routine, and prepare the space in which you're going to strip.

> *Tell your lover that it's alright to look, but not to touch.*

Remember to enjoy the experience – stripping isn't just for your lover, it's also a chance to show off your sexuality and enjoy the attention. And if your lover sees that you're enjoying yourself, he'll be able to sit back and enjoy the experience too.

The look

Choose something that you know will turn your lover on, whether it's a thigh-skimming schoolgirl skirt or a showgirl outfit. Wear layers so that you've got plenty to take off. Wear shoes and accessories such as thigh-high boots or gloves that go up to your elbows – anything that can be slowly peeled off. If you're going for a schoolgirl look, a tie is a sexy addition to your outfit (and it can be used later for some mild bondage!). Make sure all your clothes come off with ease – clothes that slip or slide off – or ones that can be slowly unzipped – are sexy whereas catches or fiddly buttons that take time and concentration aren't. When it comes to underwear, choose something you know your lover likes or go for the traditional stripper look of fishnet stockings, suspenders, G-string, and a sexy bra.

The venue

Decide where you want your lover to sit or lie, and where you're going to perform. If you want to give your lover a front and a back view of your body, position a mirror behind you. If you're feeling nervous, low light can boost your confidence – use the dimmer switch if you have one, or light some candles. Alternatively, if you're feeling confident, you could turn all the lights off and set up a single spotlight. You might also want to use a chair as a prop. You can sit on it back-to-front so that you're forced to sit with your legs wide apart. You can also rest your foot on a chair while you slide your stockings down your leg – this gives your lover a tantalizing glimpse between your legs. Make sure you set up your music in advance.

Once you've stripped for your lover, try dancing for them too. When you're down to your underwear, sway and swirl your hips to the music. If you feel self-conscious, just close your eyes and concentrate on feeling sexy.

Dirty dancing

Dance towards your lover and when you're right in front of him, place one foot on the floor between his feet and the other on the bed (or on the arm of his chair). Stroke and caress your body and run your hands up your legs to your thighs. Lean over your lover so that your breasts almost touch him, but not quite. Tease him by pulling away if he tries to touch. Now straddle his legs, and move your hips in a way that simulates sex. Turn around and sit on one of his legs. Lean forward, hold onto his knee, and move slowly back and forth.

Throughout the performance move away from your partner and dance for a few moments, allowing him to see your front and back, then move close again. Occasionally, make eye contact and smile (think sexy thoughts as you do this). The image you're projecting is one of sexual self-confidence – you're enjoying your own sexual power and you're totally in control. A sexy dance is more about attitude and confidence than about dancing skills or having a perfect body

Lap dancing

Lap dancing and pole dancing has lost its seedy reputation. Instead it's seen as a form of sexual self-expression that's fun for both watcher and watched alike. If you don't have a great deal of confidence in your moves, you can even take lessons. Here's one man's account of his relationship with a professional lap dancer.

"I couldn't help myself – I got very excited by her dancing."

"I was at a party in a friend's house where one of the guests was a lap dancer. She was very attractive and uninhibited. She had very few clothes on – and even less as the night went on! We'd been looking at each other and she smiled at me a few times. Eventually, she came over and we started talking.

She asked me and my friend if we would like a lap dance. My friend said 'no', but I just thought: 'why not – go for it'. She swayed and danced in front of me, then she leaned right over me so I could see her breasts. The way she moved was very sexy.

I just couldn't help myself – I got very excited by her dancing,
although I could have done without my friends watching. After
the dance we went back to partying. But at the end of the evening
we slept together.

That was the beginning of a very raunchy relationship. She was bright,
outspoken, and extremely comfortable with her body. She stripped
and danced for me – I think it was the fact that she seemed so self-
assured that made her so sexy. I thought I had gone to heaven.

One of my best evenings was when she came to my office. I'd had to
cancel a date with her because I was working late. She arrived looking
very conventional in jeans, trainers, and a raincoat. But then she took
her clothes off. She was wearing a black lacy basque and stockings and

"She kept brushing up against me and then pulling away again."

She thought she was going to have to work hard to lure me away from my desk and so she did a very playful lap dance. She kept brushing up against me and then pulling away again. We ended up having sex on my office chair. That was a first for me! I hope none of it was recorded by the security cameras.

Ultimately, the relationship didn't last – probably because I was too jealous and couldn't cope with the fact that she did lap dancing for a living. But we stayed extremely good friends and she really opened my eyes to the pleasures of being performed to!"

Having sex in front of a camera can add a fun, risqué dimension to your lovemaking. You not only have the enjoyment of sex, you have the thrill of watching yourselves afterwards. If you've ever fancied yourself as a porn star, here's your chance.

Porn star

Just a word of warning: before you make your erotic movie, check that it is just for the two of you and no-one else. Once you are captured on digital camera or mobile phone, there is the possibility that you can be beamed around the globe. Trust between the two of you is essential.

How to make an X-rated movie

- If you're not comfortable with filming a particular sex act or a particular part of your body, tell your lover in advance.
- Hold the camera in your hand during sex, or set it up on a tripod. If you do the latter, you'll need to make sure that all the action happens in one place.
- If you've never filmed yourself before, just shoot a small amount of footage and then watch it back. It will quickly be clear what works and what doesn't. It will also become clear whether you feel comfortable looking at your body on screen – this can take some getting used to. You may decide that erotic film-making is not for you.

Oral sex is more erotic when it is shot at close range and you can really see the action.

- If you're going to use props or sex toys, such as vibrators or dildos, get them ready in advance and keep them within grabbing distance of the bed.

- Keep changing the action or the angle from which you are shooting. Missionary position sex shot from the same angle for 10 minutes can be boring to watch later on.

- Close-ups are more exciting and intimate than long shots. Oral sex and penetration, in particular, are more erotic at close range when you can really see the action.

- Think about a soundtrack: do you want music playing or just passionate moans?

- Hook your digital camera up to your television as you record yourselves. It will feel like a porn film going on in the background. It will also enable you to monitor what is being shot so that you can change the action if you want to.

- If you feel daunted by the idea of making an erotic movie, dress up and take on characters. It's often easier if you're pretending to be someone else. If one of you is more exhibitionist than the other, make them the centre of attention.

- Make movies with different moods: slow, loving, and sensual or fast, passionate, and wild.

The thrill of power games comes from the absolute vulnerability of one partner and the absolute dominance of the other. Play power games over the course of a whole evening, or even a whole day.

Power play

Do what I say!

Decide who is going to be submissive and who is going to be dominant (read how to be a good dom or a good sub on page 70). Now all the dom has to do is to start issuing their demands! Here are some suggestions:

♦ Lie down on the floor and beg me to have sex with you.

♦ Give me 15 minutes of oral sex.

♦ Dance for me naked.

♦ Get on all fours so I can spank you.

♦ Lick me all over.

♦ Feed me food with your fingers.

Of course, if the submissive partner fails to deliver, punishment must be administered. This could mean torture by ice cube (use your imagination!) or binding your lover's wrists, stimulating them to near-climax, and then leaving the room! Of course, you release them later!

Seducing your lover in an unusual location can be a thrilling experience, particularly if you habitually make love in the bedroom. People often fantasize about sex outdoors or at work. The potential for being discovered can be a potent aphrodisiac.

Sex in unusual places

According to one UK magazine survey, 60 per cent of people said that they had had sex in a public place. People often fantasize about sex on a beach, or in a forest, or field – there's something sensual about lying on grass or sand, feeling the sun on your skin, or gazing at the stars.

If you live in a town or a city, novel locations for sex include car parks, stairwells, lifts, and offices. You need to be adept at spotting opportunities for privacy and for having quickie, stand-up sex.
One sex trick is to have part-private, part-public sex by keeping your clothes on and leaning out of a window – this works best if you're high up, say in a hotel room looking down on a busy street. He enters her from behind and keeps his movements small and barely discernible.
Be aware that having sex in a public place means breaking the law!

Sex party

HOW WAS IT FOR YOU?

"He bounced into the room and said, Come on everybody... take your clothes off."

"I was single at the time. On the invitation to the party it said: 'Bring a bottle and an open mind. Dress code: provocative. Strictly adults only.' That was enough indication that this wasn't going to be an ordinary party.

When I arrived things seemed fairly mundane. Everyone was standing around talking and drinking wine. Then the host, who is known for his exhibitionism, bounced into the room wearing a thong and said, 'Come on everybody, what are you waiting for? Time to take your clothes off.'

He said it in such a humorous, unthreatening way that people seemed happy to do what he asked – and, after all, that was what we were there for. Some people stripped naked; others just down to their underwear. I took off my clothes bit by bit.

The atmosphere of the party changed pretty quickly. People became much more familiar and relaxed with each other. The sexual tension started to build as well. A few people laid down on the floor and the sofas to talk intimately with each other. I got into an extremely flirtatious conversation with the host. 'Come on,' he said, and led me to the bedroom. It was all so open I didn't have time to feel nervous.

We stayed in the bedroom talking, kissing, and touching for ages. Gradually, other people came and joined us. The bed was massive and there were at least two other couples sharing it with us.

"Everyone seemed to be kissing and touching. Some were having sex."

Everyone around us seemed to be kissing and touching. Some people were having sex. I was so uninhibited by this time that I simply watched and wondered. It's the only time I've ever been able to see other women having orgasms. I felt completely intrigued.

I can only liken the experience to an intense playtime for adults. I never did it again, partly because I started going out with someone. But I did, with my partner's knowledge and permission, meet the host of the party on another couple of occasions. He is quite an exceptional human being."

Pleasure party

If you throw a pleasure party your guests may well remember the experience for years and, in some cases, for a lifetime. A pleasure party can be anything you want it to be – an occasion where people strip off or dress in erotic costumes, or it can be a full-blown orgy.

Whatever you decide, inform your guests of what they should expect in advance. Surprises can be fun, but offending your guests isn't.

Create a relaxed, intimate atmosphere for your celebration. Keep the lights low, the music sexy, and the air fragranced with incense or essential oils. You can decorate your house in a humorous or a sexy theme. Different rooms can have different themes:

♦ Make the kitchen a shrine to food sex (leave out plenty of whipped cream, honey, ice cubes, and soft, sensual red berries such as raspberries and strawberries).

♦ The living room can be an erotic cinema. Stage a screening of classic erotic films such as *In the Realm of the Senses*.

♦ The bedroom can become a sensual den. Cover the floor with cushions. Light some candles. Leave out massage oil and erotic books such as illustrated copies of the *Kama Sutra* or erotic massage books.

People often feel self-concious or reserved at the beginning of a pleasure party because they're not quite sure what to expect (or what will be expected of them). The solution is to provide plenty of funny, sexy, playful ice-breakers. Here are some ideas to get people relaxed, talking, and in a sexy frame of mind.

◆ Hand out exotic masks (such as gold or silver Harlequin masks) to guests at the beginning of the party.

◆ Serve cocktails with two straws in each glass. Tell your guests that they must find a partner with whom to share their drink. Give the cocktails sexy names.

◆ Ask guests to anonymously write down their favourite sexual fantasies/sex positions/experiences in a book. Leave the completed book in the bedroom or bathroom for guests to read at their leisure later on.

◆ Play games such as pass-the-parcel but with an adult twist – the prize in the inner parcel is a sex toy.

◆ Have competitions: the funniest/sexiest/silliest lap dance or strip, for example. Give naughty prizes.

◆ Play party games in which the loser must remove an item of clothing or do a sex-themed forfeit.

◆ Write chat-up lines on pieces of paper (the cornier the better) and drop them into a hat. Get each guest to pull one out and find a partner to try it out on.

◆ Lead by example: if you want your guests to take their clothes off and get amorous, start the ball rolling yourself!

Surveys of people's favourite sexual fantasies show that making love à la trois come is a regular chart-topper. If this is a fantasy that you would like to turn into reality, here are my tips for making a threesome work. In my view, having a warm, friendly relationship with potential lovers is preferable to an impersonal, anonymous, one-off, group experience. This allows you to build trust and intimacy.

Three's company

I was once asked to be in a threesome by a couple who paid no attention at all to me during the evening. Surprise, surprise, I was not interested. Their technique was faulty, to say the least.

Before a threesome make it clear that anyone is free to slow things down, take a break, or withdraw completely at any point. Never force anyone to do anything. Ease into a threesome gradually by massaging each other and simply being playful, friendly, and affectionate.

Divide your attention as equally as possible between your lovers. You all need to feel desired, valued, and included. Feelings of jealousy and exclusion are why things can fall. Above all, enjoy experimenting.

Threesomes often end up happening with a close friend of a couple. As long as the friend feels comfortable and neither member of the couple feels jealous or threatened, this kind of threesome can be fun. Here is one woman's account of a night in bed with her lover and her best friend.

Me, my boyfriend, and my best friend

"My best friend and I have always been very close and intimate and we've often shared a bed together. Sometimes, when we've been at parties, we've kissed each other for fun, but nothing more. Lisa gets on really well with my boyfriend, Peter, and the three of us often spend weekends together.

One night Lisa came round for the evening and we were all lying on the bed watching television together. There was a film in which two women snogged each other. Peter said, 'Why don't you and Lisa do that?' Lisa and I laughed and said 'no problem'. But unlike our other kisses this one went further and we both realised that we really enjoyed doing it.

The three of us started fooling around on the bed. We spent a long time taking turns to kiss each other or trying to kiss each other all at once – it was very silly and playful. Then Lisa suggested that we should take our clothes off. By that point the three of us were really turned on, so we did.

"Lisa and I kissed and caressed each other as Peter had sex with me."

We each had a turn at receiving a massage from the other two. And we stood up with Peter in the middle and gave each other a group hug. Then I lay on my side with Peter making love to me from behind. Lisa and I kissed and caressed each other as Peter had sex with me – it was incredibly erotic and orgasmic for all three of us.

One of the reasons that a threesome worked is because we all know and trust each other. I wasn't worried that Pete and Lisa would run off together afterwards and I wasn't worried about sex impacting on my relationship with either Peter or Lisa. We had a laugh about it the next day and even though we haven't been back to bed together we've kept that playful intimacy going – and we're very flirtatious when we're together. I am glad we experimented – I feel as though I've done something special."

For many people anal sex is a regular part of their sex
life. For others it remains an occasional activity. If you're
a novice, there are some guidelines to follow, the most
important of which is: go incredibly slowly – anal sex isn't
something you can rush. It's also essential to use a large
amount of water-based lubricant.

Anal sex basics

Tell your lover that you're going to start by giving her an anal massage
with your hands and that she can ask you to stop at any point. Cover
your hands in lube and use your fingers to stroke and circle the entrance
to her anus. Gently push your finger into her anal entrance – keep
stroking and circling to encourage the muscle to relax. When your lover
is ready, insert a second finger into her anus to help it to open up. Slowly
and gently push your fingers deeper inside her.

If your lover is comfortable with two fingers inside her, ask her if you
can put your penis in (apply more lube at this point). If this hurts her,
either withdraw, or stay still until she relaxes again (don't push harder!).
Ask your lover to stroke her clitoris – the more aroused she is, the easier
anal penetration be. Finally, a word of warning: anal sex is technically
illegal between heterosexual adults in several countries and states.

Hiring a lover

For some people, paying for the services of a professional lover is a liberating, not to mention exciting way of achieving sexual intimacy. Here's one woman's description of what it was like to hire a man for the night. A word of warning (especially for women): invite someone into your home only if you feel sure you can trust them.

"He advertised himself as a boyfriend for the evening."

"A friend of mine told me about this guy who advertised himself as 'a boyfriend for the evening'. She knew a woman who had hired him for a sensual massage. I was at a point where I'd had been out of a relationship for six months and I was at a low ebb and really wanted physical touch. I asked my friend if she could get this guy's number.

He sounded really nice on the phone and we arranged for him to come over the following night. He was young and quite boyish-looking. He was dressed casually, and he seemed very relaxed and at ease with himself.

He took charge straight away. He suggested that we had a bath together. At first he sat on the side and bathed me, then he stripped off and got in too. Afterwards, he wrapped me in hot towels, cuddled me, took me to the bedroom and gave me an amazing massage.

At no point did I feel hassled or pressurized. He made it clear that anytime I wanted to stop all I had to do was say the word. Paradoxically, it made me shut up. He was very skilled at massage and I felt all the tension slowly going out of my body. I started feeling very relaxed and sensual. I just wanted him to go on and on.

And he didn't stop at body massage. He moved on down to my clitoris and, when he'd aroused me to an almost mindless pitch of excitement, asked if I wanted him inside me. I had just enough presence of mind to say: 'What about a condom?' He had one ready. When we were

"He was very skilled at massage and I felt all the tension going out of my body."

having sex he carried on using his hands to massage my breasts, belly, and clitoris. It was pretty amazing. I forgot about the fact that I was paying for sex – it felt more like a one-night stand.

Afterwards, we cuddled for a bit before he got out of bed. He was totally friendly and business-like. Because it was just about sex and I didn't feel an emotional connection with him, I didn't mind him leaving. He was a real professional throughout the whole thing. I don't know whether I'd do it again, but it's certainly an experience I won't forget in a hurry."

Sex and shopping

5

Going shopping for sex toys with your lover is a great way
to get more intimate – choosing what to buy means talking
about what you like and don't like in bed. Sex toys not only
ramp up your arousal levels and enhance orgasm,
they can also make sex feel more playful
and adventurous.

Your taste in toys

EROTIC INTERVIEW

Is your lover a novice or an expert when it comes to sex toys? These questions are designed to get you talking – there are no right or wrong answers.

1 If you were going to give me a sex toy as a present, what would you choose?

2 If you were in a sex shop, which section would interest you most: dildos and vibrators; penis pumps, rings, and sleeves; anal toys; strap-on harnesses; or bondage gear?

3 Have you ever tried G-spot and prostate gland massage using sex toys? If yes, what was it like? If no, would you like to?

4 Would you use a double pleasure vibrator with me? (A double pleasure vibrator is one that consists of two connected but separate devices – a vaginal vibrator for her and an anal vibrator for him.)

5 If we had a sex toy box under the bed, what would it contain?

Listen to and learn from your lover's answers. What is their attitude towards sex toys? Are they reserved yet curious, wildly enthusiastic, or somewhere in between? And which bits of the body are they most interested in stimulating – on themselves and on you?

Sex toys for her

Ever since Samantha of *Sex in the City* extolled the incredible virtues of the rabbit vibrator, sales of this sex toy have rocketed. The rabbit vibrator consists of a large penile-shaped projection, with a round squashy part at the base filled with small balls. You insert this projection into your vagina, and the balls stimulate you as they rotate. Also attached to the base is a second, smaller protuberance with feather-like fingers (they look a bit like a rabbit's ears). This moves in a way that stimulates the clitoris very precisely. The result is that you feel stimulated by several different kinds of sensual movement.

G-spot stimulation

If you enjoy G-spot stimulation, but find it difficult to get your fingers in the right place, a vibrator with a specially designed curved tip can help. Move the vibrator up and down the front wall of your vagina to find the place that yields the most intense sensations. The better vibrators pulsate instead of vibrate, and some vibrators do both. The G-spot reacts best to the pressure of pulsation rather than the friction of vibration. If you prefer static pressure on your G-spot, the best sex toy for you is probably a dildo with a curved tip.

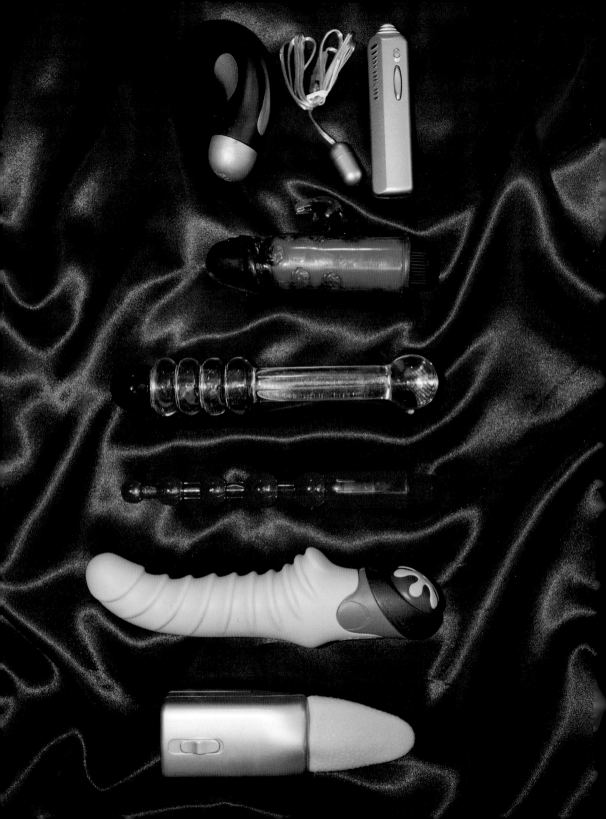

Double penetration

If you like being penetrated vaginally and anally at the same time, double-ended dildos can do this. A double-ended dildo is designed so that one end can be inserted into each orifice. Alternatively, some devices consist of a standard dildo with anal beads attached to the end. You can also buy vibrators designed for double insertion. And if you want clitoral stimulation too, look for a device that has a third protrusion for the clitoris.

A vibrator gives you an extra blast of clitoral stimulation.

Clitoral stimulation

If you find it difficult to come from penetrative sex alone, a vibrator gives you an extra blast of clitoral stimulation. The problem with most vibrators, however, is that their phallic shape makes them difficult to wedge between your and your lover's bodies as you have sex. One solution is to use a clitoral vibrator that is designed to be worn on the man's penis; the other is to use a special, ergonomically designed vibrator that curves around the woman's pubic bone and vibrates against her clitoris.

A word of warning: never dust your sex toys with talcum powder after cleaning – talc has been linked with cervical cancer.

Close the door to your bedroom and abandon yourself to an hour or more of sensual and erotic indulgence – with the help of your favourite sex toys. Give yourself plenty of time and make sure that you won't be interrupted. Here's how one woman spends her Monday mornings.

Masturbation Monday

As soon as my husband leaves for work, I bathe myself in the tub with lots of frothy bubbles and sweet-smelling soap. Then I go back to bed, which still smells of my husband from the night before. I get my special vibrator out from the side drawer.

This gorgeous toy is quite capable of getting me to climax in less than a minute, but I usually want to take things a bit further than if Keith were present. It's a special sexual treat for myself – I'm free to do whatever I want at whatever pace I want. It complements my sex life with Keith.

Then I get my anal vibrator out. Because it's specially designed for anal use, I can insert it with no fear of it disappearing inside me. I use tons of lube on it and I push it very slowly and carefully into my anal entrance. I have to be very relaxed and aroused to do this, so I usually stroke my

clitoris or caress my breasts and belly first. When the vibrator goes in, it gives me a feeling of great fullness and helplessness.

The next thing I do is to insert the rabbit into my vagina and make sure the tickly clit feathers are in the right place. Then I switch on both vibrators. One of my favourite fantasies at this point is of being completely helpless because I am being held down by several men all desperate to have sex with me. The sensations quickly become overwhelming – it feels like there's so much stimulation going on. If I'm in the grip of a powerful fantasy, I actually have to try to stop myself coming too fast.

> *"When the vibrator goes in, it gives me a great feeling of fullness and helplessness."*

I try to let the sensation build and build. Eventually, I feel totally vulnerable and I kind of explode into orgasm. After that I feel so super-sensitive I can't move fast enough to turn the sex toys off. Then I let myself drift off into a bit of a trance. When I feel ready, I get out of bed, wash the vibrators in the bathroom and get on with the rest of the day. It's a great method of meeting the morning's challenges!"

Sex toys for him

The range of sex toys for men is growing. You can buy everything from a pair of lips that massage the penis to an anal plug that stimulates the prostate gland.

Penis pleasure

The classic masturbation toy for men is a penis sleeve. It's designed to surround and enclose the penis as you thrust in and out – some sleeves provide focused vibrations too. The quality of sensation varies between models, so read product reviews before you buy. Features to look for are a tight, snug fit, and material that feels good to the touch – some sleeves use a material known as "cyberskin" that has a stretchy, tactile quality. You can buy penis sleeves in the shape of an anus or a vulva – some are more tasteful than others!

There's one design of penis sleeve that looks like a huge pair of luscious juicy lips. When you penetrate this mouth you discover that inside is a very talkative tongue that massages while it chatters.

The testicles are an erotic zone that, until recently, has been mainly forgotten by sex toy designers. Now, however, you can buy a vibrating penis sleeve that contains bumps on the inside and tentacles around the edge specially designed to tickle your testicles.

Some men enjoy using a penis pump during masturbation – you insert your penis into a cylinder and then pump the air out of the cylinder to create a vacuum. This, in turn, encourages blood to rush into your penis, giving you a strong erection, plus the eroticism of a tugging sensation on your penis. Penis rings also give you a full erection – you put them on the base of the shaft and this produces a pleasurable feeling of tightness and traps blood inside the penis. Some penis rings come with a vibrator attached or an extra ring to go around the scrotum.

Pulling anal beads out at the moment of climax intensifies orgasm for some people.

Anal pleasure

Many toys are designed to be inserted into the anus. Some of them move, vibrate or can be bent into the shape of your choice. Look for an anal stimulator that is designed with male anatomy in mind. Some anal sex toys have one protrusion that is perfectly angled to hit the prostate gland (the male G-spot) while a second protrusion massages the perineum. Anal beads are also very popular – a series of beads are inserted one by one into the anus (they are attached by cord) and then pulled out. Pulling them out at the moment of climax intensifies orgasm for some people.

If you want to give yourself and your lover a sexy treat, spend an evening trying out a range of sex toys. Your assignment is to assess each one on its individual merits. Here's one couple's experience of a weekend of experimentation.

Robert and I decided to buy a load of sex toys to experiment with at home. We went to our local erotic shop... we bought five balls, vibrators, a vibrating cock ring, and penis nipple clamps and a double-ended dildo.

Rating sex toys

We took them with us on a weekend away. We had a great time indeed trying them all out. I think my favourite was the purple rabbit vibrator. Robert's favourite was the mini beaded one with a bit of the veins of the rabbit thing... but also cool.

One problem was that when the rabbit was lubricated it had quite a strong chemical smell. But when I turned it on the vibration was fantastic and the effect worked immediately. I always felt a bit cheated because I climaxed so quick. But I stopped caring about the chemical smell, and in fact I started to associate it with feeling really turned on.

Robert has always had a fantasy about anal penetration – I don't think he'd go as far as saying he wants anal sex. But he was definitely into trying the anal beads. We were both really turned on after giving each other oral sex and I massaged his perineum and anus with my fingers. I used loads of lubricant on him and then inserted the beads one by one. While Robert masturbated, I gently moved the beads inside him. When I knew that he was about to come, I pulled the beads out quite slowly. He said it was a powerful sensation.

> *"I loved the vibrator with the curved tip. I had very strong waves of pleasure."*

I also loved the vibrator with the curved tip. Robert held it inside me – it was intense. It definitely did what it said it was going to do – which was to target my G-spot. I wouldn't say it was orgasmic exactly but I had very strong waves of pleasure – it felt very sensual and blissful. Robert also used the vibrator to massage my body and breasts which felt very sexy.

We used the sex toys again after that weekend but the rabbit and the beads are the only ones that we use on a regular basis. It was a great theme for a dirty weekend. In fact, we're planning another one. The next thing that Robert wants to try is a butt plug that stimulates his prostate gland."

Some sex toys are designed for solo pleasure while others are made for the two of you. Experimenting with sex toys is a great way of adding not just intimacy and passion, but also humour and frivolity to your sex life.

Toys for two

◆ The love swing – this is a swing that you suspend from the ceiling. It comes complete with stirrups, and back and bottom supports. The theory is that you can achieve a whole new range of sex positions while suspended in mid-air.

◆ Strap-on harnesses and dildos – if you want your hands free while you penetrate your lover with a dildo, a harness is the sex toy for you.

◆ A cock ring with an attachment – a cock ring fits around the base of the penis and keeps a man's erection firm. Cock rings come with all sorts of vibrating attachments that are designed to stimulate the woman's clitoris during sex – find a design that works for you.

◆ Sex furniture – you can buy stages, wedges, and ramps that will turn a room into a sex playground. Sex stages have fittings that allow you to tether your lover during bondage play; ramps and wedges allow you to have sex in novel positions.

◆ Double-ended toys – one end goes in her and one end goes in him. Look for double-ended dildos or vibrators.

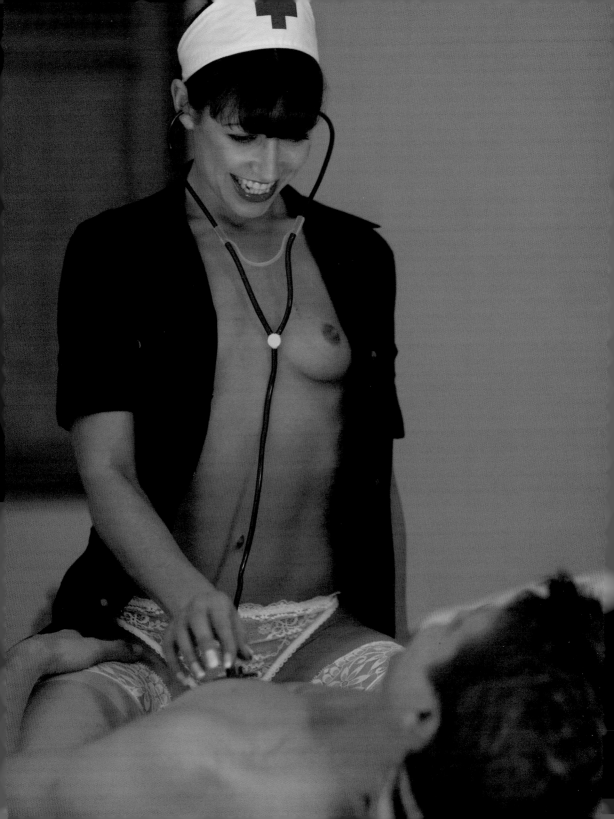

Playtime

Sex toys have great novelty value, but when their immediate thrill has worn off, it's time to get creative and incorporate them into a game.

Fish tank

Fill an empty goldfish bowl with slips of paper, each nominating a different sex toy in your collection. Every evening, as you come in from work, pull out a slip of paper – that's the toy you will use tonight.

Doctor and patient

It's examination time and, as the doctor, you need to assess the effect of different sex toys on your lover. Which ones make his heart beat faster and his breathing quicken? Which ones take her to the peak of arousal and make her come more quickly than usual?

Gender bender

Have a transgender evening in which you swap clothes and take on each other's sexual role. Get out your toy box and select some lubricant, your favourite dildo, and a strap-on harness. Women: some strap-on harnesses are designed to be worn with vibrating cock rings that will give extra stimulation. An alternative to a harness and dildo is a prostate massager – you operate this by hand.

There are some basic ground rules that should always be applied to sex, especially when you are experimenting with sex games, toys, or roleplay.

The rule book

Firstly, make sure you trust your partner. If you have any anxieties about a partner or potential partner, do not go ahead. Wait until a time when you feel more trusting or less anxious. And act responsibly yourself; if your lover doesn't want to do something, don't manipulate them or force them into doing it.

It's also important to give plenty of time to sex. If you or your lover find an area of sexual experimentation difficult, you don't have to give up straight away. It is possible that you just need more time. Slow things right down and discuss what kind of pace suits you both. In sex therapy there is an infallible rule: if some aspect of sexual activity feels wrong, just go back a stage.

Finally, have care and consideration for your partner. One of the problems with exploring new aspects of sex is that the sex itself can become too important and the partner or the relationship somehow dwindles by comparison. If that happens, insist on bringing the focus back to your relationship. If you don't, you risk losing intimacy.

Safer sex basics

It's important to protect yourself from HIV (human immuno-deficiency virus) and other sexually-transmitted infections if you are sexually active. This means wearing a condom during intercourse or having non-penetrative sex (stimulating each other by hand, for example); and avoiding rough sex that might break your own or your lover's skin. You can also reduce your risk of infection by avoiding casual sex.

Make sure you know how to use a condom correctly before you have intercourse, and always take care when putting a condom on. Condoms can be damaged by sharp nails or oil-based lubricants. Squeeze the air out of the tip of the condom before you unroll it down the length of the penis. Many sex toy manufacturers also recommend putting condoms on sex toys such as vibrators and dildos before use.

Make sure that you always clean sex toys carefully after use. Unwashed sex toys can harbour bacteria. Toys made of cyberskin are best washed with specially formulated cleaners. Silicone toys can take washing with mild soap, and jelly toys are best cleaned by wiping them with a damp washcloth. Always take the batteries out of sex toys before washing them.

Index

Acknowledgements

For clothing:
Honour (Latex wear)
86 Lower Marsh
London, SE1 7AB
020 7401 8219
www.honourclothing.com

MASTER U (Leatherwear) Ltd
Unit 52 Camberwell
Business Centre,
99-103 Lomond Grove,
London, SE5 7HN,
020 7708 5474
www.masteru.com

Torture Garden Clothing
(Latex wear)
Unit 30, Cremer
Business Centre
North Entrance, 3rd floor
37 Cremer Street
London E2 8HD
+44 (0)20 7729 7714
www.tgclothing.com

For sex toys:
Johnny Horn (for him)
Freephone (UK) 0800 915 6635
www.johnnyhorn.co.uk

Sh-womenstore (for her)
57 Hoxton Square
London N1
020 7613 5458
www.sh-womenstore.com

Love Honey (for her)
freephone (UK) 0800 915 6635
www.lovehoney.co.uk

For photography:
Ruth Jenkinson, John Freeman